Inner Dialogues

Salient Voice

BookLeaf Publishing

Presentation by *BookLeaf Publishing*

Web: www.bookleafpub.com

E-mail: info@bookleafpub.com

ISBN: 9789357442190

First edition 2023

I dedicate this book firstly to myself. Thank you for being dedicated to the gift that was placed in you. Most importantly this is to you, the reader, as you take in the pieces of my world into yours.

ACKNOWLEDGEMENT

I am so thankful to God, because writing a book was something that sat on my mind, but I didn't know when that would happen. So, to see my first collection of poetry come together is surreal!

I am thanking me, for my consistency, commitment to my craft and seeing myself through #TheWriteAngle challenge.

Thank you to my family who support me in things I set my mind to do, their backing is everything to me! I love my OgiloEmpire so much! Migwo!

To my home skillets (I just made this up) aka my friends who support me constantly with my poetry and always rooting for me, I love you all.

Thank you, BookLeaf publishing, for #TheWriteAngleChallenge it is another steppingstone towards me honing my craft and stepping out of my comfort zone.

Finally, thank you to you, yes YOU, the beautiful human who decided to purchase this book and spent some pounds regardless of the economic crises, you are so appreciated, and I couldn't be any happier! This book is for us, and I just pray a poem relates and encourages you!

Thank you!

PREFACE

Each poem is a combination of emotions that were felt and inner thoughts which have been turned into words to relate to each reader. One page could be the only thing that relates to you and that will be 100% okay.

I have been told my joy, scars, words, and life experiences, individually and collectively can connect with someone in such a unique way that I have never imagined.

Therefore, I have written these poems in the order that I have. Every day I had something to share that I wrote with vulnerability, uncertainty, a smile, trust, and humility in mind.

"Life gets real, thoughts and emotions are not always permanent, but I pray through the pages you find what is REAL and AUTHENTIC to you".

FREE

Let her reintroduce herself because she hasn't
seen you in a long time,
Your worlds have been kept apart.

Myopia, is why she hasn't been able to truly
receive you because when it is being shown to
her face, It is clear, evident, but when she is
being told hers is coming, that it's on its way,
her vision is blurred.

It is capped from reaching any further than arm's
length.

Doubts have been playing the game of squash,
two opponents battling for the win.

There appears to be no exit point within the four
walls of her mind
Her opponent is not here for an easy game, it has
been hitting with such ferocity
It wants everything she has; its beginning tactics
is to steal.

So yes, it has stolen a lot more than a few
It stole you; it diminished your strength in her life
It took away from her freedom to see and her wisdom to strive.
Stagnant became her dependency hidden under a veil of pretence that she is fine.

So, yes, please, let her reintroduce herself to you freely with no doubts.

"Hello faith, nice to meet you, I am free, so I accept you, I fan you to set you ablaze. I am new to this so teach me how not to easily separate myself from you."

KEEP SEARCHING

The grip
The clutch
Holding onto dear life
Making sure every clasp lasts
Hoping every second lasts a little longer
Searching for ways to make sure this stays
forever
Eyes closed, squeezed a furthermore, hope just
got closer.
So, you reach into your inner man so external
noise can be shut out
Highest focus is on the grip, the intentionality of
being present just to get further
Reality will try to take your moment, dim your
light, blur the vision just to limit your sight
But don't let it, keep searching, keep finding the
'you' that lays resting within you.
How many more steps, how many more tests, so
many unknown stairs
Hold firmly to that handle because this quest is
yours to win.
Eyes open, more alert in vision, freedom is here.
A moment of stillness to embrace you
Make sure every moment counts.
The squeeze

The hold
It all depends on you.

THE AUDACITY

I have not given you a spirit of fear

An unpleasant, often strong emotion caused by
anticipation or awareness of danger

A basic, intense motion aroused by the detection
of imminent threat.

Both sentences have not been given any type of
audacity.

Its referred to as basic, the audacity!

A False Evidence Appearing Real

Yet, I still have this false evidence wrapped
around me
Its lies comforting me like I asked it to.

I am subject to its voice, like I don't have one
stronger

My mind is wired to its noise, so I constantly see
myself smaller.

Why?

What shifted in my brain waves?

What acceptance letter did I sign before the tides could wash this all away?

Why do I put fear so high on such a pedestal?

Why do I elevate them like they belong to the sky?

Why do I give them the same privileges that the birds possess?

Why do I praise them like they are the Prince of peace?

When they only cause destruction in our inner man just to see us lose a piece of our identity.

Fear, the audacity

You have no right to belong in headspaces, to be allowed to speak so profoundly.

You will be sick of this mouthpiece!

You hate a rebuttal!

You hate when I come at you!

You loved the times I just allowed you to play peak a boo with my certainty

Just so you can pick and choose when to show up and make me so frantic.

Fear, I'm taking back what you took from me

You hate action,

Movement, against your very words spoken

You hate that and that's exactly what I am going to do

Fight you with actions done in truth!

Serve you with your eviction letter, pack your lies in whatever suits me because I am done with this case, I am taking you straight to the Judge, He will lay you out straight!

Because before I was formed, He never gave me a spirit of fear, but He gave me one of strength, of love and of a sound mind.

So, our friendship ends here.

FIRST TIME

There is always a first time for everything.

Everything that now lives, had a first time before
it got to where it is now.
Even God's creation had a first time,
When He instructed earth to arise from its
slumber
To wake up and prepare for the mission that it is
about to encounter.

It was shapeless and empty
There was no life to it, unheard of it seems.

Then God coloured earth, texturised it with
various landing and gave it a wider space
He gave names to things and places, He used
light to form seasons, days, and years.
Yes, earth's first time was a whole vibe.

Although not all first times we experience are
going to be fond memories
Like the first time your little toe got familiar
with the foot of your sofa
The first time you had to put a plaster on your
heart because of an ex-lover

First time mummy introduced you to the hairdressers
First time you said your final goodbye to that family member and the first time you received a no in something you were hoping for.

First times can be a toughie, the churning in your stomach
The stomping thoughts that rush through your mind or the coming of a silent whisper that gently increases in volume.
The demeanour in which your face takes, it's evident something was at stake because now you are left with a feeling that you can't shake.

Earth's first time has its negatives, but it is still craved
Like the first time you made a new friend
The first time you tasted ice-cream, the glow in your eyes, unless it made you intolerant
The first time you met God, just perfect, heaven sent or the first time you took a leap of faith, and it all went well.

The first time in anything can be very daunting
But it holds the key to memories that will last a lifetime.

First time is like deciding to finally act on
something you have held back on for years
The quietude your body, mind, and soul reaches,
it's nothing that can be bought but something
that must be sought after.

First times are key lessons, undertake it,
understand it, and earn it as flying colours under
your belt.

MOOD WAVES

You come in like mood waves,
Draining everything around me.
You come in like mood waves,
Draining everything around you.

On a spectrum you don't balance it out
And it's our energy you're draining out
You're forgetting that what you give out is what you receive in
Making your moods determine how you feel
drains you especially and everyone else.

It's not easy to remind myself that I must sit up straight,
Appear prim and proper, with a smile and eye contact before I start serving my mood waves on a cold platter.
I must pull my cheeks slightly up
Even when my world sees mostly frowns.
Be aware of other people
Even when I push back on my needs.

I am a force when my spectrum is on the far left
It's hard to unlock it.
I am present but not entirely in the room

I use iron gated fences to encircle my mood.
My actions, louder than my voice
My hands and feet know this, so they carry my
mood and my face bears witness.
It takes me to release the hold it has on me or for
my mouth to speak me out of the feeling because

It comes in like mood waves
Leaving its remnants for me by the shore.
When I adjust myself to the middle of the mood
spectrum
I'm grounded again but I am left with the
aftermath of my mood hurricane.
Hoping I could rewind time and not drain my
energy on a thing that fluctuates
But it is too late.

Because it comes in like mood waves
Draining me and everything around me.

TIMING

POV YOU:
Are we there yet?
Are we there yet?
How long till we're there?
When will we be there?
Are we there yet?
Wait, I hoped for now….
Okay…
So
Are we there yet?
Noooo, I do trust! I do, I do!
Okay
Erm
Erm
So, it's not like…I don't trust…
Okay, no nothing.
Erm…
Alright, are we there yet?

POV God:
"Child, breathe, I am working, whilst you have been speaking, I have been working, I just need you to keep trusting Me. My timing is everything. It comes in perfection, and it is never late or too early but it is right on time,

when you need it the most. Wait on Me, you're doing just fine and yes, child, BREATHE"

P.S
I love the power of timing, it's a teacher and a rewarder.
I choose to trust it no matter how difficult.

NEWNESS

A time will come where experiencing newness is required in life
A time will come where taking yourself out of your norm will feel strange
but it will confirm everything you didn't realise you utterly needed.
The flashbacks of holding back moments will visit your present as a reminder to keep pushing
Joy will fill the atmosphere as you breathe in and appreciate each hour.
You will merry go round with patience
Holding firmly your hands as you tour guide on new grounds.
Your smile will copy the sun, whilst your glow becomes radiant.
Your movements will dance like the ocean, sure of where it has been
with no limits to where it will go.
Like birds you will soar, your mind will reach higher places it has never witnessed before.
Your palm will mind its business and push boundaries for generations to come
You will break cycles that appeared difficult.
Newness is on its way
Get ready, stay ready, and don't let it pass you by.

THE COOKIE JAR

Today…I hit a brick wall
Thinking I was off it.

I find myself dipping my hand into the same cookie jar I promised myself to stay out of.
I love the taste so dearly If I am to be real
It is like having a sweet tooth for something that isn't good for you
I have tried to ignore you, like how some of us ignore the elephant in our rooms.
I have it sat right in the corner; plain eyes should be able to see it, but no one notices.
It frequently pops its head out to remind me that "I am still there"

I have been told to keep the jar out of site so it's out of my mind but it is easier said than done.
Why does constant repetition of the same thing feel so natural when you know it's not good for you?
Why does finding yourself in similar situation like your elders, even though you swore to deviate from that same pattern, feel like it was always meant to be?
It's weird.

This cookie jar is calling out to me like it was sent on a mission
One that can't be terminated until its target eliminated
Yet it never dies.

How can I distract myself from it, find it less appealing so I don't have to suffer the consequences.
I remember the first time I tasted those cookies, everyone knew about these
It was talked about, easy to access and sold on every shelf.
The beauty about these cookies is that they are pocket size snacks
However, that same feature also makes it, its worst
It makes them super addictive, reaching and needing another bite of its goodness
Why do they have to taste so delicious?
Why do they have to linger that moreish taste in your pallets?
Just why?

I keep hitting that brick wall whenever I stay away from it
It's like the adrenaline rush comes heavy and I consume more than I should have

Then It's followed by unwarranted guilt spoken at me

"Thought you said not anymore, because they add stones to the thighs?"
"Thought you said you are done with it, and you look elsewhere if it catches your eyes?"
"Thought you said you will find a replacement habit and not let it have you on a chokehold?"

Well, I guess, I will just put all of that on hold

Because today I hit a brick wall. It makes me think if I choose to stay away from the cookie jar again, when next will I fold?

UNFILTERED

Today I felt deeply
I started a few lines and stopped
I wrote nothing in full.
It was a reflective day for me
The last day in a foreign country
Amongst other things, this is the one thing I
chose to share with you

Why does the location impede the ability of
being 100% yourself?
"Go ahead be you, you'll never see these people
again anyways"
Why can't it be normalised that we are who we
are authentically even if we see these people the
next day?
Why does the location matter?
Or if there are familiar faces in the area?

A question only you can answer:
Are you, You, regardless of where you are or
who is around?

FALLING

How is it that I am falling and not getting caught?
I have taken my safety net and put it in my own hands
The same hands that are gripping onto my disappearing breaths
I can feel the air wanting to leave my lungs and my mind slowly shutting down.
How have I kept my own catch on my watch?
When there is a Son that wants to embrace me every time I fall?
I am proud and that's the reason I am sometimes stagnant.
I think I can do it on my own and be independent
Maybe it's just a childhood unresolved issue
Where being independent came at an early stage
So, in adulthood it's only right to keep that action in motion.

How is it that I am falling and not trying to rescue myself?
I have put my coping mechanism on auto pilot that it just recycles itself time and time again

To soothe my painful moments but it's a
detriment to my future
I am slowly losing balance of holding it all
together versus giving it all to Him.
So, I find hiding my speciality
Invisible cloak to hide all my flaws
But the beauty is that He sees through it all.
But I find hiding easier whilst He seeks me
To remind me that He is with me.

How is it that I am falling and not allowing Him
to do His work
Leaving His perfect Will to run its course
through my being
As He provides everything I need.
There must be a way to stop myself from falling
Because I am failing repeatedly
I use my own strength to set myself free
It works a little while but no longevity.

How is it that I am falling and not getting
caught?

THE GOOD AND THEN THE BAD

We have heard the spirits speak
The good and then the bad
Choices are ours so they are still to be made.
Middle ground
Hanging on the defence
Luke warming in a fiery place
Uncertainty through life's piercing fang.
Do you choose to stay ablaze in this cold world?
Certain of where you stand
Walking in the narrow lane?
The choice is yours.

DEEPER THOUGHTS

Having deep thoughts amidst a joyous
environment is something.
It's not tangible but it is a thing that deprives
you from living in the moment
Living in the palms of regrets
Threading on the lines of lies
Having whispers that are familiar to your
eardrum.
It doesn't tip toe around you, but it forces you to
tip toe in your own mind.
Bring yourself down to a miniscule
But, at any time, if you chose to stump,
disconnect with those vicious thoughts it loses
its power.
So, what does it do, it keeps you strangled,
wrapped in the webs of deceit
Feeling like you are out of reach.
It clenches its claws into your membrane
Leaving you playing those ideas on repeat.
It gives you five reasons as to why it has you
trapped
One, because it has made a promise to come for
everything that you've got

Two, because you were falsely lured into a marriage with self-doubt, so why would you be given an easy way out.
Three, because it knows your strength, so why would it allow you to be you? So, it keeps you bound in the middle.
Four, because its aim is to point out all your flaws, making it all you focus on even if they are true or false evidence appearing real
Lastly, the fifth reason being that once you're set free you have the ability to hold and pick yourself up, because the strength lies within you.
However, all it does in joyous moments, is rob you of your peace, it forces you to sink, to get deeper in your feelings.
In this joyous moment,
There are smiles around you
Laughter's aroma is in the air
Good energy transmitted through every conversation
Yet, it has you paralysed in your own skin.
Having this happen so often it
It has come to my attention that a decision is all you need to bring yourself back to reality.

Choosing to get out of your head and leave behind the chaos that tries to rob you of your joy.

SHALOM

They thought I was worthless
By the way their eyes scanned my actions.
They put aside their own shortcomings so they could focus on mine.
They decided on their own accord that I was made perfect so that means I should not make any mistakes or be shown grace.
They put on blinders so that they can look through their own lenses, not Yours.
Their actions demanded I should be okay with their scrutiny, but their words made it seem like they weren't looking into me, oblivious that You have been made aware of my weaknesses.
Wolves in sheep clothing they appeared to be.
They took distance like the most important thing
You would think I had leprosy with the divide they caused amongst the people because I went astray.
Hypocrites You called them
Pharisees if we should get biblical.
They separated their understanding of the true meaning of mercy,
The true meaning of love,
The true meaning of transparency.

They thought I was worthless
So, when I took all that was mine and left
I won't be surprised if they had a party in my absence
They thought my sin was contagious, but they don't know how widely spread their brainwashing has been.
Go on, question them and they would speak that in prayers my name will be mentioned and that my return is one they have envisioned.
When a place can no longer be called home
You don't return there like the prodigal son
Instead, you find a new house and make it home, find your Father, get deeper on your own
Surely, that's fine?
Well, is it?
To an extent, because then you start fighting the thoughts of being worthless right after they robbed you of our innocence.
Yes, with that, I know it can never be seen as home.

They thought I was worthless
I can't event fault this because I started to make it my identity
I carried a label that wasn't designed for me.
It wasn't part of His blueprint
So, I knew I had to come clean because I stole it and started to play colouring

I started to create my own lanes and pencilled in
ways I thought my life should be
Because I took on an identity that wasn't for me.

But
Everyday I'm learning "no regrets just lessons"
I'm learning "pray for them and inject
forgiveness"
Because when memories have been stamped in
your memory
It's difficult to move past it when they appear in
your present.

They still think that I am worthless?
Who cares?
I know I don't.
Home is in my father's palms and everyday I'm
reminded that I was worth it, I
am worth it and I will be worth it.

Shalom.

STILL

I am putting my ears close to the ground
I am paying attention to every sound
Intentional with every move
Obedient to every word that speaks

Pin
Drop
Silence

So, I can grab every wisdom You give.

JEREMIAH 29:11

Let Me fall lightly in your hands
Catch every drop of Mine.
With your hands gently curved like two C's
meeting at a centre point
Permit the lines on your palms to lead Me to
your withered grounds.
Allow Me to refresh your soul, can I?
For I know your unique path.
The plans I have for you in mind, goes further
than the sky
Further than the ends of many oceans combined.
My plan is
To hold onto you continuously,
To water you with hope,
To make prosperity your coverage,
Far from bringing harm to you but to meet you
with a future.
My plan is to be with you till the end even when
the rain doesn't stop
So, you can see it as showers of My blessings
because even in the lows I'm still present.
So, permit the lines on your palms to lead Me to
your withered grounds
So, I can refresh your soul if you let Me.

CHECKING IN

I know, I am meant to pick up my bags, the
pieces and keep it moving
But in my own reality I live on a daily, I am
faced with more than what your eyes can see.
I hide more than what I physically show.
The saying you are the only one who truly feels
what you are feeling in the moment
Beams like the red stop sign at night.

CHASING

Today, it dawned on me that I find myself
chasing what is next
I live in the present and simultaneously have my
past pulling me rapidly.
I don't want to get stuck looking back at what
has been
In a way, some will say that's a good thing!
I find that I don't look to my past to really
appreciate it
Not wanting to look or think back to past
memoires
In my mind, if I do, it means I will be reminded
of negative experiences.
So, I need to keep flicking through to find the
good moments
Whilst I do, I see enlarged thorns in the process,
sharp turns which caused me heart aches, a note
that someone left, decisions made that caused
me to close the gate.
Looking back can be frustrating, but the journey
goes on.
So, I found happy moments in lost and founds,
untendered shelves
I found moments where I felt so much joy and in
me being proud of myself.

Looking back isn't always a bad thing,
especially when done with intent.

I was reminded today that my past, the good
memoires are to be cherished
I can hold on to it, I can learn from it.
Yes, I find myself chasing what is next, but I
must find time to appreciate what has been.

GOD's GIFT

This one is for you Ese,
Dedicated especially to you.
A star amid darkness
Your light isn't out
Your light still radiates.
If there is life
Hope still breathes.
You and perfection aren't cut from the same
cloth.
Shortcomings doesn't exclude you, it's part of
nature
You aren't the worst when you come to this
junction
You learn from it and keep it pushing.
Strength was weaved into your frame
Right from the foundation, your roots take
grounds, they aren't withered or dehydrated.
So don't take for granted what flows freely
through your veins.
You have the strength of a warrior
Your hands have been tied, yet you still find the
path to freedom
You are God's gift wrapped in melanin skin
A voice that is unique to your being

You tell stories lived directly from your shoes
and ones given to you by Him.
Your best is yet to come
Don't let the past tie you down to what has been
Don't let people be what limits you from living.
You are no longer a caged bird so feel free to
sing
Admittedly, not the best singer, but your
harmonies are your very own melodies
One that isn't for everyone
You are not for everyone, that is in fact a good
thing.
You're a fighter, one that doesn't give up easily
Use those hands to keep taking what has your
name labelled on it.
Keep your eyes on Him, humility at His feet
That's where your grounds hold moisture don't
forget this.
He gives breath to your branches, so they bare
fruits accordingly.
You were wonderfully made, so your beauty
takes home in His eyes.
Ese, everything you're seeking is found in you
He provides it all.
This one is dedicated to you
The one who started a good thing in you is sure
to complete it.

DISTANT PAST

Distant happenings that make the present
distorted
Distant pain that makes the present painful
Distant decisions that make present movements
bound
Distant days that should face death but lives
presently
Distant sad experience that limits your present
happiness
Distant holds that makes your present words
choke
Distant times that make your present slow.

Letting go is difficult
I know I should because the pain eats at my soul.

Someone said "it's hard to get your gifts and
blessings from God when your hands are full"
I have been storing, treasuring my past like
souvenirs
So that cut me deep because it's the truth.

Now, I'm choosing to settle my past
For my freedom and for my future self.

THERAPY

The struggle of going against your Will
A worst enemy, disguised as working in your favour
Soothing you in the moment, then taking the ground you stand on.
It fights your corner and then backs you to the corner shortly after.
I have been dining with my flaws repeatedly
Is this the table where the enemies are sat?
Where I am the only one serving?
When is it my time to eat and be merry?
Surely this shouldn't be how it is.
Balance is key.

I'm throwing away my diamonds and collecting broken stones for the price of my peace
Believing in what people on the outside say about the inner man in me
And when you've walked through life people pleasing you start to think it's your reality
Failing to dissect me delicately.
I blame certain childhood encounters
Friendships that sat high on pedestals
It took multiple breakups to learn the truth

To also see some ugly truth in my reflective
view.
I have seen a man's action bring out my worse
reaction
I promised myself to never allow man to stoop
me so low
So, I protect my worst to keep my best at my
forefront.

Balance is key.

I've been playing hopscotch with my self-worth
Throwing my best into empty spaces
Keeping my balance to not focus on my worst
traits.
Life throws curved balls that I try to dodge
I fight hard to not lose my balance in the race to
get what's mine
But I keep taking a few steps back and finding
myself at the starting line

Again.

Balance is key

Keep the momentum up, don't lose the key
To life, I must learn to breath
Count to 5
1

2
3
4
5

Release

The struggle to go against my will
I must put an end to it and watch it take me to
places I once didn't believe.
Change the narrative
Let it build a stronger person in me.

Balance is key.

Willpower works actively
But the spirit in me yearns fervently
So, I must find balance when pouring into me.

Balance is key.

BEYOND THE STUFF

Movement must proceed
Action must be taken
Hope must live on and not die
All this, amdist all the stuff
And beyond the stuff.

Clouded around are thoughts of insecurities
Received from negative experiences
Some self-inflicted from personal choices or repeated actions.
I'm my worst critique so when I stare into their eyes
My attention span increases leading me to take fewer actions
But like waves in the sea, I don't quit, my body still permits movements
1% a day is my minimum but not my limit because

Movement must proceed
Action must be taken
Hope must live on and not die
All this, amdist all the stuff
And beyond the stuff.

I gaze into midnight stars
Observing one particular heavenly body
Pondering if wishing on a star will make all my dreams come true.
But wishes are for childish gimmicks.
Hope is where reality is
So rather than wishing on a star
I find myself working relentlessly when the sun sleeps
The moon and I understand one another
Because we shine even in the darkest hour.
Mentally, physically my mind stays creating because

Movement must proceed
Action must be taken
Hope must live on and not die
All this, amdist all the stuff
And beyond the stuff.

So, I let my faith rise
I dream again because there's a pot of gold awaiting me.
I chose to live again
I am looking, constantly searching within me
Putting aside old lame excuses
Swapping them for His undying promises.
No longer waiting for anything to be handed to me

With my right hand I take possession of
everything that's mine because

Movement must proceed
Action must be taken
Hope must live on and not die
All this, amdist all the stuff
And beyond the stuff.

www.ingramcontent.com/pod-product-compliance
Lightning Source LLC
Chambersburg PA
CBHW051740130826
49812CB00033B/942
* 9 7 8 9 3 5 7 4 4 2 1 9 0 *